PEOPLE, PEOPLE, PEOPLE
A BRIEF HISTORY OF NEW ZEALAND

Stevan Eldred-Grigg

David Bateman

Page 1: James Smetham, *The New Zealand Chiefs in Wesley's House*.
Above from left: J J Merrett, *Young Maori Man of High Rank, Whakatane*; William Fox, *St George's Bay, Auckland. Mr Blackett's House*; Evelyn Page, *New Year Holiday (Corsair Bay)*, detail; Olivia Spencer Bower, *Rawene Mothers*.

Text © Stevan Eldred-Grigg, 2011
Typographical design © David Bateman Ltd, 2011
Images © individual contributors

First published in 2011 by David Bateman Ltd,
30 Tarndale Grove, Albany, Auckland, New Zealand

www.batemanpublishing.co.nz

ISBN 978-1-86953-813-2

Text design and layout: Alice Bell
Maps by Nick Keenleyside, Outline Draughting and Graphics
Printed in China through Colorcraft Ltd, Hong Kong

CONTENTS

New Zealand Centennial Exhibition. Artist: L C Mitchell.

Map of New Zealand

NORTH ISLAND

NORTHLAND

- Kororareka
- Whangarei

- Auckland
- Thames

HAURAKI

- Hamilton
- Tauranga

WAIKATO

BAY OF PLENTY

Waikato River

KING COUNTRY

EAST COAST

- Gisborne

- New Plymouth

TARANAKI

Whanganui River

HAWKES BAY

- Hastings
- Napier

- Whanganui

MANAWATU

- Palmerston North

- Wellington

WAIRARAPA

- Karamea
- Nelson

NELSON

- Blenheim

Wairau River

MARLBOROUGH

- Greymouth

- Kaikoura

WEST COAST

- Christchurch

CANTERBURY

- Ashburton
- Timaru

SOUTH ISLAND

- Queenstown

OTAGO

- Oamaru

- Dunedin

Clutha River

SOUTHLAND

- Riverton
- Invercargill

Stewart Island

Chatham Islands
Waitangi to Christchurch 860 km

- Waitangi

ONE

Discovery, 1200 to 1500

Islands without People

New Zealand in the year 1200 was a land of trees and birds — and no people. The two main islands were covered nearly entirely in deep, dark, cool forest. The many smaller islands were nearly all forested, too. The country was home to millions of birds. Some, like kiwi, weka and the large moa, did not fly. The coasts and shallow coastal waters were alive with sea lions and seals, while thousands of whales swam in the deeper seas off the coasts.

The birds, sea lions, seals and whales had never been hunted by people. The trees had never been burnt or chopped down by people. New Zealand had never been settled by people.

New Zealand was entirely unknown to any people anywhere in the world.

From the nothing, the giving birth;
From the nothing, the increase;
From the nothing, the plenty,
The power of increasing,
The living breath.

Maori traditional song about the beginning of history.

Polynesians

Polynesians discovered the islands we now call New Zealand. They travelled more than a thousand kilometres across the ocean before finding the country. The year of discovery was perhaps as early as 1250 and perhaps later than 1300, but nobody knows the exact date. The travellers came from tropical islands: the Cook Islands, the Austral Islands and the Society Islands in Eastern Polynesia. They were farming and fishing people, and also very good sailors. Polynesians for over a thousand years had crossed the wide ocean on long difficult journeys to distant Pacific islands. They were perhaps the most skilful sailors in the world, crossing the sea in fast sailing boats called vaka or waka.

A land of forests. **Joseph Welch**, *Nikau Palm*.

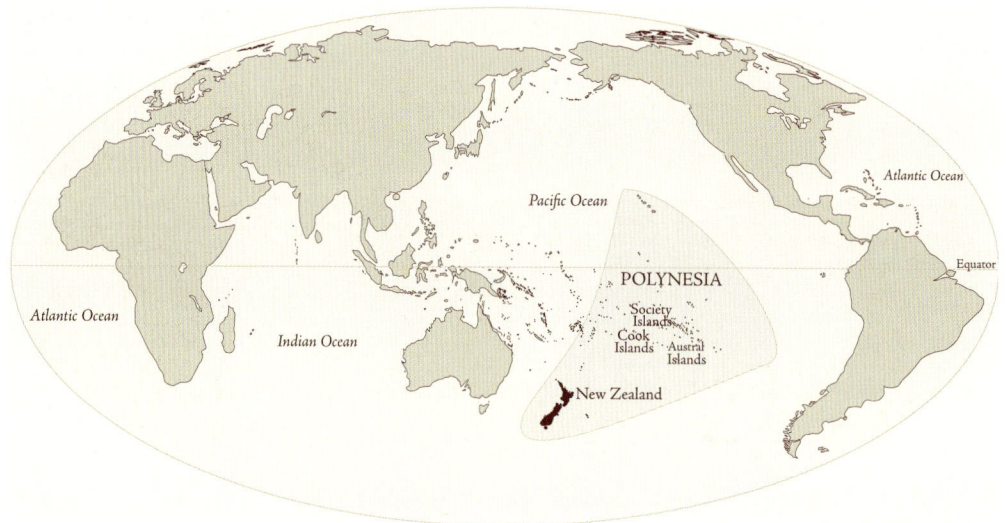

New Zealand in the World: 13th and 14th centuries.

The groups of travellers made several journeys, at different times and from different islands. Altogether they numbered perhaps several hundred women, men and very likely children, too. They brought with them food plants and animals, because they planned to settle the new land. Food plants included the sweet potato, called kumara. Animals included the dog (kuri) and the rat (kiore). They probably brought chickens and pigs, too.

Dogs and rats, together with people, quickly settled the whole country.

The speed with which they settled two very big islands and many small islands is amazing. Polynesians within about fifty years not only found and explored all the islands of New Zealand but kept sailing south. They travelled nearly five hundred kilometres into the cold ocean to find and settle, for a while, the Auckland Islands.

The settlers also travelled back towards their home islands, taking with them new things from New Zealand. Stone found in the new land and useful for tools was shipped hundreds of kilometres to the Kermadec Islands and the Chatham Islands. Travellers probably sailed all the way back to the home islands several times as well.

Wealth

The new land offered a good life to the Polynesians. The wealth of the sea and the forests had never been gathered before, which meant that the settlers were able to find plenty of food and other resources very easily. The moa and seals were not only rich with meat but not afraid of people and therefore easy to kill. Hunting was best in the South Island. Settlers seem to have lived there in larger numbers than in the North Island. The oldest settlement we know about was on a wide lake at the mouth of the Wairau River in what is now Marlborough. Villages were built on lakes at the mouths of many other rivers in the eastern South Island, and on every coast of the North Island. Southern settlers hunted. Northern settlers hunted and grew food crops. Plenty of food, gathered without hard work, meant that children grew up strong and healthy. The population climbed quickly.

Yet life was hard, too. Young women often died when giving birth, while hunting and other wounds killed many young men. Teeth wore out when people were still quite young. The settlers, like people everywhere in the world during the 14th century, did not often live long. The average age at death was only about thirty.

A type of waka used by Polynesians for ocean travel. **Alex Kennedy**, *Model Tipaerua.*

A chief in the Cook Islands. **John Williams**, *Te Po a chief of Raratonga.*

Polynesians came from small, warm islands to large, cool islands but adapted quickly. Clothing, food, tools and many other things needed to change. The food crops they brought with them would not grow in the southern regions of the new land. Only some of the food crops could grow even in the warm northern regions. The crops needed far more care, too, than in the home islands.

The settlers changed the new land. They began burning the forests. Black clouds of smoke poured high into the sky. Red flames roared across the flat lands near the coasts, and later many of the hills. Moa by the thousand ran for their lives ahead of the fierce fires. One century after the arrival of the first settlers, about forty per cent of the forests had been destroyed. The settlers killed many birds, too. The rats and dogs brought from the home islands killed more birds. The rat, worse still, also ate the seeds of many native plants.

The killing of animals was so great that moa were no longer seen in many regions perhaps within one hundred years of settlement. Fur seals were no longer seen in the northern regions within two hundred years. Forty per cent of all types of land bird in the country became extinct because of settlement by Polynesians.

Power and Society

Chiefs had been the leaders of society in the home islands of Polynesia. Chiefs were probably the leaders of society in the new land. The settlers had no written language, which means that they left behind no books about their world. They did leave behind carefully buried bodies in graves. Some bodies were buried with jewellery, others were not. Those with jewellery were probably chiefs. One of the striking things about the settlers is that they still behaved as Polynesians, even though the resources they found and the economy they developed were very different from the tropical home islands.

The economy in the home islands had been based on villages, farming and fishing. The economy in the new land was based on hunting, especially in the South Island. Yet the settlers lived in small villages, just like their relatives in the home islands. They hunted, mostly, but from the beginning they chose to build villages.

The settlers moved about constantly, too, just like their relatives in the home islands. A village was home for a few years. Afterwards, the people would pack up, leave, move elsewhere and build a new village. Villages were bases, from which people went out to camps where they could stay for short periods to go hunting, or to gather other kinds of food, or stone, wood or other resources.

These Polynesian settlers were the mothers and fathers of the modern Maori.

Polynesians told their history with songs, poetry and marks on the body. The complex marks on the face of this Maori chief tell us a lot about the history of his family and tribe. **J J Merrett**, *Young Maori Man of High Rank, Whakatane.*

PEOPLE, PEOPLE, PEOPLE

TWO
Villages, 1500 to 1750

Classic Maori

The two main islands and all the smaller islands by the 16th century had been explored thoroughly and used thoroughly. Eastern Polynesians had developed into Classic Maori.

The number of people living in the southern regions grew smaller after the killing of most of the seals and all of the moa. People moved north, where the climate was warmer and they could grow their tropical food crops. People were forced by the lack of easy meat to turn more and more to foods that were hard to gather or hunt. Wild crops

A lakeside pa. **G F Angas**, *Motupoi Pah and Roto-aire Lake, Tongariro in the Distance.*

were dug up, among them roots rich in sugar from ti, a tree later known as the cabbage tree. Small forest birds were hunted. The dog and rat were cooked and eaten as food. Fish and shellfish became important foods, too. One village near Karamea, on the West Coast of the South Island, began to depend heavily on a shellfish, pipi. Centuries passed during which the village built up a hill of shells. Other villages, in other regions, often based their economy on one main sort of food.

Forest burning continued. Waikato people set fire to a forest in the late 15th century, for example, to clear land for growing crops and gathering roots. Land was burnt again, over and over, throughout the whole period up to the end of the 18th century. Burning stopped the forest from growing back. Burnt land grew cabbage trees and other plants whose roots were eaten by people. Also, cleared land was easier to travel through than land covered by thick forests.

New styles emerged in crafts and the arts. Maori developed special uses for many different types of wood and stone. Goods were traded from one end of the country to

another, especially valuable stones. Te Waipounamu (Jade River), a name given to the South Island, showed the importance of jade, a hard green stone used for tools, weapons and jewellery. Aotearoa (Long White Cloud) and Te Ika-a-Maui (Maui's fish) were among the names given to the North Island.

Maori moved about constantly, just like the settlers during the first century. Walls of wooden posts were built around many villages, forming towns known as pa. A pa served a tribe as a fort or stronghold, and almost always was built on top of a hill, beside the sea or a river or lake or on an island, or somewhere else easy to defend from an enemy. A complex group of big pa was built in the early 18th century, for example, on the tops of many of the hills of what would later become the city of Auckland. The leader who organised the work was the powerful chief Kiwi Tamaki.

A total of about 120,000 people may have lived in the country by the end of the 18th century. Only a few thousand lived on Te Waipounamu. The great majority lived on the northern half of Aotearoa.

Women dancing.
Edward Markham,
A dance called Karne Karne or Cune Cunee.

Power

Power centred on the tribe. Almost everybody lived in a hapu, a small group of people related to one another through birth or marriage. The typical hapu was a group of perhaps twenty or fifty, or at most about a hundred people. The group lived and worked together, with its own chief. A hapu often gathered together with a few other hapu to carry out special projects. One project might be the building of a pa. One project might be the fighting of a war. One project might be a hunting journey. All were chosen freely by each hapu, and were carried out for a certain period. Afterwards, people would go back to their own village.

All hapu belonged to a tribe, known as an iwi. Iwi were sometimes very strong, with many hapu. Other iwi were small and weak. Weakness could bring disaster in war, and war was widespread during these years. Tribes fought for mana, meaning authority and status, and for utu, revenge. They fought with mere, patu and other short weapons made of stone, bone and wood. Long wooden spears (taiaha) also were used to strike the enemy.

Shaking the spear
Is charging, is flying,
The twin-bladed shark,
And the foot steps beating
Oh, angry the foot steps
Blood-wet the foot steps
Bound for the world's end.

Maori traditional song before battle.

A tribe lucky in war owned many slaves. A tribe unlucky in war lost children, women and men, who became slaves of the enemy. Slaves, who had almost no rights, were at the bottom of tribal society. Ordinary free people were in the middle of tribal society. Chiefs were at the top. A man or woman became a chief by being born the son or daughter of chiefs. A chief could gain more mana by behaving in a clever way, or by being an effective leader, speaker or poet. A chief could lose mana by failing to be skilful, by failing to be effective or by being lazy. A man, or less often a woman, of lower rank could rise in status to become a chief. They could do so by being gifted or skilful in poetry, speech, politics, war or some other way. Chiefs had the right to lead, but not the power to make people follow.

Maori were not tied to their land, forced to obey the orders of lords. They were free and, although led by chiefs, they did not need to follow orders. All travelled often, and travelled widely.

Two chiefs. **James Barry**, *The Rev Thomas Kendall and the Maori chiefs Hongi and Waikato* (detail).

Young women.
Augustus Earle,
Amoko, Eana,
Hepee.

Religion breathed life into everything. Maori religion was based on a belief that there were many gods and that all living things were related to one another. Gods, while powerful, were not good or bad. They behaved much the same way as people. People had to work hard to please gods but also could try to trick them. Maui, a clever hero famous among all Polynesians, was half-man and half-god. He used his intelligence and his courage to take many powers from gods, giving them to people. He fought and defeated the god of the sea, Tangaroa. He fought and defeated the god of the sun, Ra. He fought the god of death, who was a woman, Hinenuitepo.

'Is she as strong as the sun?' he asked his father. 'I trapped him and beat him. Is she greater than the sea, which is greater than the land? Yet I have dragged land from it. Now let us see whether we will find life or death.'

Hinenuitepo defeated him, however, for she was very strong and therefore the lives of all people end with death.

The tale of Maui and the gods was passed on from generation to generation through storytelling and singing. Maori still had no written language. Literature took the form of prayers, speeches, songs and poetry.

Women and Men

Maori society was gendered, or in other words the roles and behaviour of women and men were quite different. Women on the whole had less power than men. A woman could be a chief, yet most chiefs were men. A god could be a woman, yet most gods were men. Women held the power to invite men to tribal meetings, yet men were the only people with the right to speak at most tribal meetings.

Men fought in wars, worked with wood, planted crops, rode in waka and wrote most prayers. Women worked with cloth and clothing, looked after crops, and wrote the words and created the music for most songs.

Girls seem to have been allowed less food, clothing and shelter than boys. Graves show that the average woman or girl was weaker and more bent than the average man or boy. She died younger than the average man. The number of women in any tribe was smaller than the number of men. Baby girls were often killed because they were seen as worth less than boys.

Gender, however, was not sex. A man if he wished could dress and behave as a woman. A woman could dress and behave as a man. A word widely used for lovers of the same sex was takatapui. Songs and works of art celebrated their sexuality. Maori society allowed a wide sexual freedom in many other ways. A husband could easily divorce a wife; a wife could easily divorce a husband.

Maori had their own ways of living. They believed in their gods. They believed in the land, the sea and the sky. They believed, above all, in people.

Ask me what is the most important thing in the world.
I will reply: it is people, it is people, it is people.

Maori saying.

War dance.
T J Grant,
War Dance.

20   PEOPLE, PEOPLE, PEOPLE

THREE
Europeans, 1750 to 1840

Floating Islands

Maori, looking up from their villages, gardens and fishing nets, stared out to sea. They saw something strange. Small islands floated on the water. Above the islands were white clouds.

The floating islands were ships from Europe. The white people sailing them would soon be known as Pakeha.

Two ships came as early as 1642, flying the flag of the Netherlands. The captain was Abel Tasman. Afterwards they sailed away. Other ships began arriving in 1769 from Britain and France. Jean de Surville was captain of the first French ship, while the first British captain was James Cook. Maori met the travellers, tried to talk with them, traded, played, made love and sometimes fought. Hore-ta-te-taniwha was one of many small boys impressed by Cook.

He was a very good man, and came to us – the children – and patted our cheeks, and gently touched our heads. His language was a hissing sound, and the words he spoke were not understood by us in the least.

The ships kept coming.

French, British and other Pakeha came first to explore, but from the 1790s they came to make money. They wanted the furs of seals and the oil of whales. Fur and oil were the first big business in New Zealand. Sealers worked in groups of men, employed by companies, mainly in the southern South Island. Millions of seals were killed. The peak period for sealing ended around 1810, after which the industry died out quickly. Whalers then began to settle along the southern and eastern coasts of the country. They worked, like sealers, in groups employed by companies. Tens of thousands of whales were killed for oil. The whaling industry peaked in the 1830s and afterwards, like sealing, began to die out.

Villages, known as 'stations', were built by sealers and whalers in safe ports and at river mouths. Pakeha workers lived in the little villages. Maori women who married them began to give birth to a new generation of children who were both Maori and Pakeha.

LEFT: A whaling station. **Walter Bowring**, *Jillett's Whaling Station on Kapiti Island.*
LEFT, TOP: Church and house at a Christian station. **James Wallis**, *Wesleyan Mission Station at Waingaroa, New Zealand.*

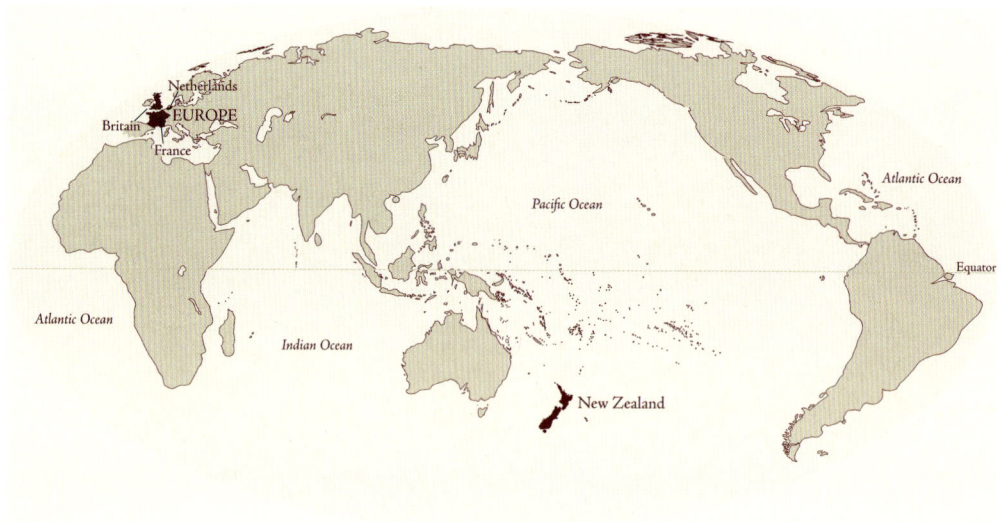

New Zealand
in the World: 1750
to 1840.

Edward Shortland described the village of Riverton, where he found cottages with white walls and fields of grain 'smiling'. He sailed up the coast to other villages. The cottage and farm building of one farmer were as neat as 'pictures', he wrote. The farmer was married to a Maori woman, who was 'dressed like a European country girl'.

Traders began to arrive, too. One trade was in flax, a tall tough grass whose fibre was valuable because it made fine clothing and very good rope. Wood, works of art and other goods were also bought from Maori. Maori bought tools, food crops, cloth and new weapons from the Pakeha.

Churches sent priests and ministers after 1814, hoping to spread the Christian religion among Maori. British and French, they built churches and villages. Crowds gathered to listen to them talk, for Maori enjoyed discussing the new religious thoughts. They were not often convinced, however, by Christianity. Priests and ministers worked to spread reading, writing and some other western skills among Maori. The skills were so useful that they were adopted quickly.

Pakeha came as guests and sometimes were attacked by Maori. On the whole, however, the new people were welcomed because they brought useful things and ideas that seemed interesting. Maori were happy to trade, talk, make friends, make love and marry Pakeha. Pakeha were happy to trade, talk, make friends, make love and marry Maori.

'I found that the natives and Europeans lived on very good terms,' wrote Shortland, 'as, in fact, appears to be the case at all these stations.'

A new crop. **Cyprian Bridge**, *View of an Ordinary New Zealand Pa with Potato Plantations Around It.*

ABOVE:
The spread of reading.
J J Merrett, *Woman and Child.*
ABOVE, RIGHT: Maori chief with servant.
G F Angas, *Ko Nga Waka Te Karaka or Clark, Christian Chief of the Nga Te Waoroa Tribe, Waikato and Wahauenuku his Attendant Boy.*

Musket Wars

The tribes governed themselves, as before, taking orders from nobody. They also kept going to war with one another. War was far worse than during earlier years because of new western weapons. Muskets and other guns were bought by some tribes from Paheka traders and used to win battles with other tribes who fought with traditional weapons. The people of defeated tribes were killed or eaten, or else were driven into slavery.

The Musket Wars began about 1818 and finished about 1830, killing perhaps twenty thousand Maori. The Ngapuhi tribe, in the northern region of the country, was the first to get large numbers of muskets. The tribe fought three wars against traditional enemies in Taranaki, Hauraki, Waikato and the Bay of Plenty. Te Rauparaha, a brilliant chief of Te Ati Awa, fought battles in the lower North Island and then attacked the Ngai Tahu tribe of Te Waipounamu. The experience was later described by a defending chief, Tuhawaiki:

He went through us, fighting and burning and killing. At Kaikoura, at Kaiapoi, and at other of our strongholds, hundreds and hundreds of our people fell, hundreds more were carried off as slaves, and hundreds died of cold and starvation.

The wars ended only when all tribes had muskets.

Foreign Illness

Guns were not the only cause of mass killing. Death swept through the country because of something much smaller: bacteria and viruses. Pakeha diseases had a severe effect on Maori. Before contact with the new people most Maori were rather healthy. They had not been exposed to many infectious diseases from the rest of the world and therefore had no natural protection from new types of illness. Sexual infections, for example, now not only killed many women and men but caused blindness in babies. Pakeha did not intend to spread disease among Maori. Doctors understood very little about how such diseases were spread anyway. Yet the effect on the people of the country was as great a disaster as the Musket Wars. Twenty thousand or more people were killed.

Colony of New Zealand

Maori looked for new ways to deal with the damage caused by disease and war. Thousands began joining churches and taking up Christianity. Chiefs spoke about grouping tribes together to protect the independence of New Zealand. A few northern tribes in 1835 signed a Declaration of Independence. European governments accepted that the Declaration was legal under international law.

New Zealand stayed Maori.

Maori were not as strong as before, thanks to war and disease, but they still controlled the country. Pakeha were few and weak. The lives of all, however, were about to change. Hundreds of thousands of Pakeha, coming by ship to the islands, would transform New Zealand, bringing with them sheep, steel and steam engines.

The first wave of new settlers came in 1840 on the ships of two companies formed by investors in Britain and France. The British New Zealand Company planned to make money by building towns in the lower half of the North Island, along with all of the South Island. The French New Zealand Company planned to build ten or twelve towns in the South Island.

Britain decided to stop the French and try to manage the situation in the country by taking control of the whole of New Zealand.

A small group of British officials, together with many Maori chiefs, early in 1840 agreed to a document called the Treaty of Waitangi. A contract, it was offered to the Maori by the government of Britain. The rights of British citizens were given to all Maori. The British believed that the treaty gave them the right to govern everybody in New Zealand.

ABOVE:
Maori Christianity.
C D Barraud,
Interior of Otaki Church.
ABOVE, RIGHT:
Marriage between the races. The fathers of these women and children were European while the mothers were Maori.
R A Oliver, *Half Castes at Pomare's Pah, Bay of Islands.*

The chiefs believed that the treaty guaranteed Maori the right to govern themselves. The treaty also promised that Maori would keep their lands, forests, lakes, fishing rivers and their culture. The exact terms of the treaty were not clear, however, and ever since have caused disagreements. The treaty is seen by many people as the basis of the nation of New Zealand.

Britain now declared that the islands were under its control. The North Island was claimed on the basis of the Treaty of Waitangi. The South Island was claimed on the basis that it was 'discovered' by Cook. The true discovery, of course, had been made by Polynesians. The two big islands and all the small islands became the Colony of New Zealand. The colony was a new state, governed from Britain.

Yet the islands were still mostly Maori. The Maori population was about 80,000 while there were only 2000 Pakeha. Maori had far more military power in the islands than the new people, and also had control over the land, forests and other wealth wanted by Pakeha. Ships kept coming, however, bringing more and more people.

New Zealand was changing forever, and very quickly.

Treaty of Waitangi. **L C Mitchell**, *A Reconstruction of the Signing of the Treaty of Waitangi.*

FOUR
Colony, 1840 to 1900

New People

Wave after wave of settlers swept into the country. The French New Zealand Company built one town, Akaroa, before the company collapsed. The four towns of Wellington, New Plymouth, Whanganui and Nelson were built before the collapse of the British New Zealand Company. Colonists kept coming anyway, even after the fall of the companies, paying for tickets to the new colony. They came mostly from Britain and Ireland. Towns began to grow. Farms began to spread over the plains and into the valleys.

The colonists adapted their culture to the new land. They burned many of the forests, like those who had come before them, and more species of birds and other animals became extinct. Europeans wanted to destroy the trees, the bushes and the native grasses

The first settlement of the British New Zealand Company.
John Wallace,
View of Wellington Harbour from Thorndon Beach.

in order to plant the grasses and the food crops grown in Europe.

Pakeha brought many new animals to New Zealand. The Polynesians about six hundred years earlier had brought the kiore, which had killed off many plants and animals. Europeans now brought another rat, the ship rat, which within about eighty years had spread throughout the whole country. Good at climbing trees, the ship rat ate the eggs and young of many native animals. Pigs brought by the new settlers ran wild in the hills and forests, as did dogs. Sheep and cattle were brought by the ships, too.

The new people who arrived from Europe during the middle of the 19th century landed mostly on the dry, yellow, grassy eastern plains and valleys of the South Island. The forests had been destroyed hundreds of years earlier by Polynesians.

'I like this country very well,' wrote a young man, Andrew Rutherford; 'nothing but grass and wind.'

'It is a beautifully shaped country,' added a young woman, Alice Lees. 'Its *largeness* and the lack of trees strike me more than anything.'

Sheep farms were developed in the southern and eastern regions of the country. The biggest farms were called stations, like earlier sealing and whaling stations. The owners were known as 'wool lords'. Only thirty years after the beginning of the colony there were almost ten million sheep. The stations exported huge weights of wool to Europe.

Gold was found, too. The world woke up in the late 1840s to what people called gold 'rushes'. Crowds of young men left their homelands to chase after gold. Women followed, not to dig for gold but to sell food and sex and drink. The first big rushes were to California

British flag flying over the colony. **William Fox**, *St George's Bay, Auckland. Mr Blackett's House* (detail).

Chinese workers. **Edward Ashworth**, *Scene Near the Barracks*.

in the United States and Victoria in Australia. The next rushes, beginning in 1861 and lasting a few crazy years, were to Otago and the West Coast in the South Island of New Zealand. A new song was sung throughout the colony:

'Gold! Gold! Gold! Bright fine gold!'

Gold drew settlers to New Zealand from Britain, Ireland, Scandinavia and Germany. The rushes also drew another new group of settlers: young men from China. Thousands borrowed money from businessmen in southern China and came in groups to dig for gold in New Zealand.

Colonial towns grew into cities. New Zealand became one of the most modern and developed countries in the world. New Zealanders earned incomes higher on average than nearly any other country. The colony soon began to govern itself through its own parliament, established in 1853. Only men with some money were allowed to vote, however, so the young colony was governed by landowners, lawyers and businessmen who passed laws favouring the rich and the middle class.

Gold miner. **W H Speer**, *New Zealand Digger*.

PEOPLE, PEOPLE, PEOPLE

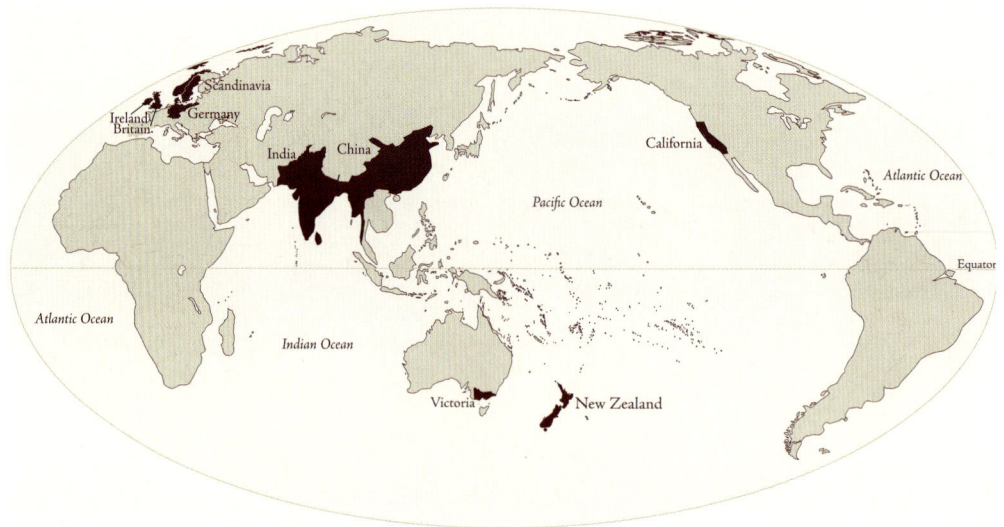

New Zealand in the World: immigrant homelands, 1840 to 1900.

A policy that suited those with money was to spend government income on roads, railways and on shipping tens of thousands more people to the colony. The roads and railways, paid for by the state, created riches for rich people. The tens of thousands of people shipped to the colony provided the rich with plenty of workers, and helped the governing groups to drive down the wages of the working class. Only about 40,000 people were Maori by the end of the 19th century, while nearly 800,000 were Pakeha.

New Zealand in this way became a 'white' or Pakeha country controlled by the children of settlers from Britain, Ireland, Germany and Scandinavia. Governments during the 1860s and 1870s paid to bring new settlers from Europe. Governments from 1881 passed laws to prevent settlement of the country by people from China and India.

The rich and the middle class proudly saw their country as a new Britain, a 'better' Britain.

War

Pakeha New Zealand was so rich and grew so quickly that the government always wanted more land on which to settle more people from more ships. They wanted Maori land. Maori, meanwhile, were not always happy with their position in the colony. Often they refused to obey the new laws brought by the British. Often they refused to sell land. A few wanted the new people to go away. Hone Heke, a chief, spoke these words to a governor:

Go back to your own land, to England which was made by God for you. God has made this land for us.

TOP LEFT: A battle in the Northern War. **Cyprian Bridge**, *Sketch of the Action at Mawe, New Zealand, on the 8th May, 1845.* LEFT: Another battle in the Northern War. **John Williams**, *Ruapekapeka, N.Z. January 1846* (detail).

The government of the colony responded by going to war against several tribes. A few small wars were fought in the 1840s, beginning with a brief battle in Marlborough. Battles were then fought around Wellington and Whanganui. The heaviest fighting followed in 1845–46 in Northland during what came to be known as the Northern War.

A period of peace followed, yet more settlers kept coming. The pressure kept growing for more land to be bought or taken from Maori. A group of powerful tribes centred on Waikato gathered together and formed a new kingdom to defend their traditions and their rights. The government made up its mind that any tribe joining the kingdom was outside the law.

New Zealand Wars. **Gustavus von Tempsky**, *British Camp Surprised by Maoris who were Driven off with Heavy Losses.*

The New Zealand Wars began in 1860 and lasted for twelve years. British troops in red and blue uniforms served as the first government weapon. Afterwards, more and more shooting and killing was done by a tough and well-equipped settler army. The government had powerful guns on wheels, too, and war ships that steamed up the Waikato and other rivers, shooting into the heart of the North Island.

Bodies were broken among bullets, shells, steam and smoke.

The power of the Pakeha settlers caused new religions to develop among Maori. A blend of Christianity with old tribal beliefs, they were a way for people to try to make sense of what was happening. Yet also the religions divided tribal society. Bitter battles were fought between tribes. Villages were burned. Women and children were killed. Men's heads were cut off in order to win a government reward.

PEOPLE, PEOPLE, PEOPLE

A last battle fought at the forks of the Waiau and Mangaone streams in Te Urewera in 1872 was followed by several anxious years when many regions seemed an armed camp. Maori and Pakeha kept remembering words spoken at one battle by a leading chief, Rewi Maniapoto.

'Friend, I'll fight against you forever, forever!'

Tribes that fought against the government lost most of their land. Pakeha soldiers were given some of that land. Tribes that fought for the government were allowed to keep their lands and often won positions of power within the state. Ngati Porou was one tribe that profited in many ways.

Laws were passed by the parliament of the colony to try to end all possibility of future wars. The Native Schools Act, for example, established a system of free schools for all children of Maori. The law seemed generous since the state at the time did not provide free schools for the children of Pakeha. Maori schools, however, attacked the basis of traditional culture and society. Teaching was carried out not in the Maori language but in English.

The law that did the greatest damage to tribal society was the Native Lands Act. The Native Land Court, set up under the law, aimed to end the traditional way in which tribes owned land as family groups. The court divided up tribal land. Land, when divided, was given to private owners from the tribe.

Private ownership made it much easier for land to be sold. Vast areas, many millions of hectares, quickly began moving from tribal ownership into private ownership, and often soon after into Pakeha ownership.

Maori tribes in most regions found the impact of war and law to be very damaging. Maori, it seemed, were a 'dying race'. William Baucke was one of many Pakeha writers who spoke about the defeat of the tribes with a mix of admiration and pity. He put these words into the mouth of an old Maori woman:

Listen, our people came from the rising sun, we are now going into its setting; we are hurrying into the night. As it gets darker we grope. The white man, who is far in the lead, calls back, 'This is the way; come along!' But he travels too fast.

Wealth

The colony was rich, yet the good things were not shared in an equal way. A wide gap yawned between the rich and the poor.

The wool industry, by far the biggest industry, was owned mostly by those who were very wealthy. Workers had little hope of buying sheep, let alone land for those sheep. The grasslands of the eastern and southern regions quickly became a settled landscape of great estates. Wool lords built elegant houses and laid out private parks. Sarah Courage, a young woman on a sheep station ten years after the establishment of the new town of Christchurch,

The house and park of a rich landowning family. **C D Barraud**, *Cheviot Hills Homestead.*

was 'surprised to find everybody and everything so civilised'. Lucy Moorhouse wrote that she and her sisters also were surprised when they arrived from Europe. They had expected a wild new land.

'We were disappointed,' she wrote, 'that it was so like England.'

Gold regions were not so settled, and nor were most regions of the North Island. Wetter than the southern and eastern regions, the northern and western regions could not be turned easily and quickly into sheep stations. They were regions of 'family' farmers. A family farm was a small piece of land owned and worked by one family. The work was hard. Thousands of family farms slowly spread through most of the best land in the North Island, and some of the South Island.

Industry began to develop on a large scale by the 1870s with the growth of factories, shipping and railways. All used the power of steam engines. One out of every five people working in the colony by 1880 was employed by manufacturing. Workers earned wages in food and drink processing factories, leather works, printing works, cloth and clothing factories, iron works and machine works.

The new industrial wealth was developed mostly by capitalists, private owners of business and land. Railways were built and operated by the state but capitalists built and operated factories and shipping. The New Zealand Shipping Company and the Union Steam Ship

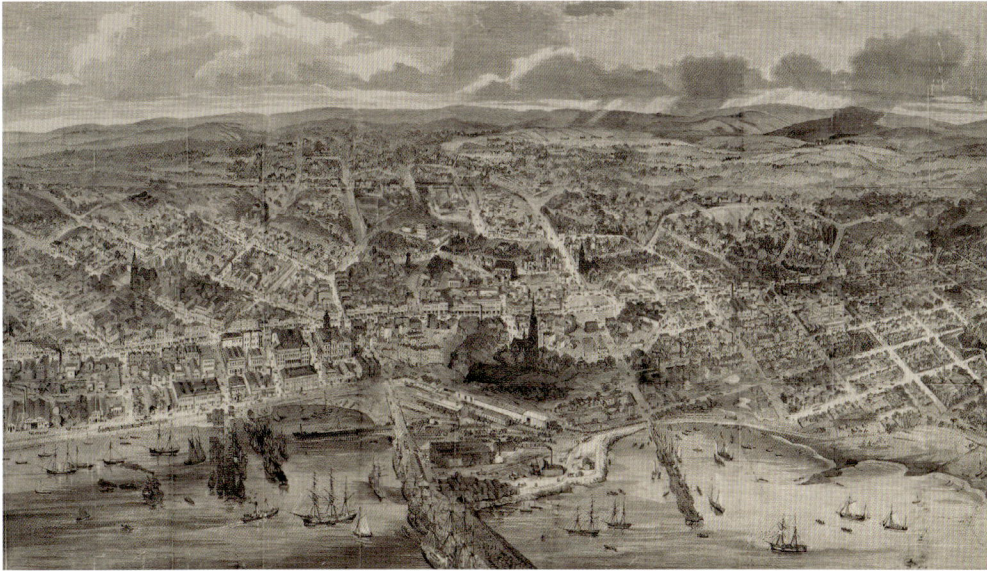

Dunedin, the largest city in the colony.
A C Cooke.

Company grew quickly and soon were running some of the most modern ships in the world. The role of the state was small in the 19th-century economy. The state usually earned no more than about ten per cent of all income in New Zealand. The remaining ninety per cent of income was nearly all in the hands of the rich and the middle class. The rich were so rich that in the year 1890 one per cent of people controlled fifty-one per cent of all income in the colony, and sixty-five per cent of all private wealth.

'The concentration of land, capital and other machinery by the few, which has taken half a dozen centuries in Europe,' wrote an American traveller, 'needed only a decade or two under the southern sun of New Zealand.'

BELOW:
Farm woman.
James Nairn.
BELOW, LEFT:
Maori village.
Charles Blomfield, *Orakei Korako on the Waikato*.

Maori chiefs visiting London. **James Smetham**, *The New Zealand Chiefs in Wesley's House*.

PEOPLE, PEOPLE, PEOPLE

Power

The wide gap between rich and poor led to a growing sense of social crisis among the working class, and also many of the middle class. A sense of crisis led in turn to a peaceful revolution. The groups of landowners, lawyers and businessmen who governed the colony from its early years found themselves slowly giving the right to vote to more and more groups of people.

Voting rights widened in most parliaments of the western world during the second half of the century. New Zealand governing groups were less willing to allow such widening than many others, changes coming about only when balances shifted between 'ins' and 'outs' within the groups. Voting rights often were less generous than in several of the nearby colonies of Australia and also France and Germany.

Men working in a factory. *New Zealand Graphic and Ladies Journal*, The Benching Room of Sargood Son and Ewen's Factory, 1892.

Maori men won the right to vote as early as 1867, which seemed very generous since the vote was denied to most of the Pakeha working class. The truth, however, was that Maori were allowed only a few seats in parliament. Gold miners also were given the right to vote. They, too, however, were allowed only a small number of seats in parliament. A step towards democracy was taken in 1879 when the vote was given to all men in the country.

The step was not as big as it seemed, because men who owned property in several different districts had the right to vote in all of those districts. This system was known as the 'plural' vote. Parliament was still dominated by rich families who formed a governing group.

A truly big step towards democracy was taken in 1889 when parliament finally, but not willingly, ended plural voting. The new principle was called 'one-man-one-vote'.

The language of class war was used widely. The government of the colony, said one group of workers, was a 'giant' animal that ate 'the working man'. Society was locked into a struggle between 'the wealthy people and the landowners' on one side and on the other side 'the middle classes and the labouring classes', declared John Ballance, who would soon become prime minister under a new political party.

'All the laws,' agreed Richard Seddon, who would follow him as prime minister under the same party, 'have been made to serve capitalism.' Revolution was spoken about widely. The colony was on the edge of 'ruin and civil war,' said a member of parliament. Yet those asking for revolution hoped to win not by violence but by means of the vote. The 'revolution will be fought,' announced a labour leader, 'with the weapons of intelligence.'

Speakers, singers and writers were busy.

Women working in a factory. *New Zealand Graphic and Ladies Journal*, The Machinery Room of Same Factory, 1892.

'I am convinced that the heart of young New Zealand, in these days, beats with free ... energy,' wrote poet Jessie Mackay.

An election at the end of 1890 brought in a government that promised a new order for society.

'For the first time in the world's history,' wrote William Tanner, a worker elected to parliament, 'Labour has taken her place of honour, and is crowned.'

The Liberal Party that now took power was based on a belief that the state should be actively involved in society and the economy. The state should take some of the wealth of the rich in order to improve social and economic democracy. The state should protect the middle class. The state should give new rights and new strength to the poor. A Liberal state was necessary, in the opinion of most of the working class and many of the middle class, to break the power of the rich, above all a few hundred families of rich owners of land. The Liberal state was said by some to be a system of 'state socialism'. Yet it was not really socialism, simply a new state involvement in certain areas of society and economy.

The rich who owned huge areas of land were the first target for the Liberals. A land tax was imposed in 1891, paid only by the owners of large estates. Income tax was introduced, too. Only the rich were required to pay it. The Liberals also gave the state the power to take the estates of the rich. Land from those estates was given as family farms, cheaply, to the working class.

Opportunities for the working class grew wider in many other ways. Factory and labour laws defined more clearly the rights of workers, and the hours and conditions of work. A new law, copied elsewhere in the western world, established a system by which employers and labour leaders met one another in the presence of a judge to settle disagreements in a peaceful way.

The state also established, for the first time in its history, welfare benefits. The Old Age Pensions Act of 1898 gave the elderly poor the right to apply for a small income, to be paid by the state.

State involvement in the economy did not grow in other ways. Overall, the belief was that a capitalist economy worked well and could offer a good way of life for everybody who was willing to work, so long as the worst harm done by the rich to the poor was kept under control by the state.

The share of wealth owned by the richest one per cent of people dropped quickly. The share of wealth owned by the poorest people grew quickly. The mood of many was one of hope. Edith Searle Grossman, a young writer, published in 1893 a novel whose title voiced the mood of many: *In Revolt*. The novel told the story of a young woman with high ideals for the future of the colony.

'Ah, those early days of a great movement!' she wrote. 'Who can bring back in later years the same intensity of life, the hope and faith?'

Children at the end of the 19th century. **Philip Presants**, *Young New Zealand at Play;
Cricket in a Mining Town* (detail).

European and American liberals and socialists visited the colony to observe the new system established by the Liberal Party.

'To sum up,' wrote a French traveller, 'protected by the law, supported by the government, commanding the vote and therefore the politics of the country, enjoying wages so high that they would make the mouths of ours water, the workers of New Zealand truly seem to have found ... the heaven of the working class.'

New Zealand had become what workers now called 'God's own' country.

Women and Men

Women and men were not equal when the colony first began, women being treated by law as 'protected' by fathers, brothers and husbands. The family life of the middle class and many of the working class was based on what some women writers and speakers began to call the 'double standard'. All property and income of a wife belonged under law to her husband. A wife could be divorced if she had sex with a man who was not her husband. A husband, on the other hand, could not be divorced if he had sex with a woman who was not his wife.

A state cannot easily police its laws about sex, love and marriage. One way to deal with unhappy married life, for example, was simply to walk out on the marriage. Many people did so. Other people often lived together as husband and wife even though they had never been married legally. The middle class did not allow women and men to behave in such ways, but relaxed marriage customs were common among the working class. Maria Eldridge was typical. She left her legal husband and took as her lover a gold miner, James Bush. They lived together as husband and wife. Afterwards she walked out on this second relationship. Why, he asked her, had she chosen to live with him as his wife?

'I was a fool, I suppose,' she answered.

Laws and moral codes changed during the late 19th century thanks to new ideas about a need for the two sexes to be equal. The most widely celebrated change, in 1893, gave women the right to vote. New Zealand was the first country in the world where women won such a right. Also the state began to protect children with new laws.

Yet while new laws gave new rights, the belief was still strong that above everything else a woman should be a wife and a mother. The belief was also strong that sexual relationships between men were wrong. Men who had sex with other men could be sent to prison for many years. A gendered view of society grew stronger, in some ways. The leaders of the working class wanted every man to win a wage good enough to support a whole family. They called it a 'family wage'. The wife of such a family could stay at home, taking care of the children, sewing, cooking and cleaning.

The middle class went still further, speaking and writing in a grand way about the woman as the 'soul' not only of the home but also the whole of society. She was too weak and pure to do wage work, let alone go into politics.

ABOVE: Young man
of the middle class.
G P Nerli, *Arthur
Hadfield Fisher.*
RIGHT:
Woman servant.
Frances Hodgkins,
untitled.

Family life in the 1920s. **H Linley Richardson**, *In Fancy Dress*.

PEOPLE, PEOPLE, PEOPLE

FIVE

Dominion, 1900 to 1950

A Lucky Land

The first few years of the 20th century were years of confidence, often of pride. Wealth gave good health to nearly every mother and baby, causing the population to grow faster than any other country in the world. New Zealand was so successful that it was a colony no more and grabbed colonies of its own among neighbouring islands, beginning with Niue and the Cook Islands. The country took a new and impressive name, the Dominion of New Zealand.

Travellers commented on the good houses, good clothes, good health of the people, their friendly manners and their relaxed way of life.

'A lucky people,' wrote one, 'in a lucky land.'

Years later, by the middle of the 20th century, the people still enjoyed very good health and wealth. The economy was booming. New Zealand was a lucky land where most people looked forward to a future of peace and plenty and more and more wealth for nearly everybody.

Yet these fifty years were deeply troubled, too. Two world wars killed and wounded perhaps as many as 100,000 young New Zealanders. A worldwide economic depression between the two wars drove many more to lose hope, to feel afraid and often to be hungry.

New Zealand went to war on a vast scale in 1914, joining the rest of the British Empire in attacking Germany and Turkey. The First World War killed 17,000 young men from New Zealand, more than any war since the Musket Wars. An army was sent across the sea to seize a new colony, Samoa. Armies were then sent around the world to occupy Egypt and afterwards invade Turkey, Palestine, Syria, Iraq, Iran and Germany. They shot guns, dropped bombs and spread poison gas. After the war they suppressed crowds calling for freedom and democracy in Egypt.

Wounded soldiers when they returned to the dominion often became a heavy weight upon their families. Wives of former soldiers struggled to hold together households in which a damaged husband could not work, or could not be happy, or could not love. Children of the war generation often grew up in houses where they needed to be careful of a mother who worked long hours, was tired, depressed and angry. Children needed to be careful, too, of a father who might awake in the night screaming, who might lose hope, who might beat them suddenly.

'Mother was very upset,' said a daughter. 'Father came home a nervous wreck. He was never again the same man she married, and the marriage broke up.'

The economy was far weaker during the 1920s than before the war, although some years were good. Afterwards in the early 1930s the world suffered from the worst economic crisis ever experienced since the beginning of capitalist history. The Great Depression, as it was called, lasted for five years. Many employees were thrown out of work. Many families became poor. Elizabeth McCombs, a member of parliament, during the worst season of the crisis estimated that as many as 240,000 people wanted work and could not find it, or were being forced to work 'only half time or part-time'. A great number of people found life hard and frightening.

Yet the economy then recovered quickly. A period began which would become known as the 'long boom', forty years of extraordinary growth and wealth. The economy grew by a remarkable seventeen per cent in one year alone before the next great crisis, the Second World War.

The war led once more to battles with Germany, and also this time with former friends, Japan and Italy. Yet again, a generation of young men went away. They fought in the Middle East, North Africa, Europe and the Pacific. Women went into the army along with men, and altogether about 200,000 people from the dominion wore the uniforms of the army, air force and navy. The government drafted most of them and almost 12,000 were killed.

The Second World War did not damage the country anywhere near as badly as the First World War. Not only were fewer men killed and wounded, the economy grew seventy per cent during the years of fighting. An advertisement near the end of the war showed a good-looking young soldier coming home and kissing his pretty young wife or girlfriend.

'This is no dream ... this time it's real!' said the advertisement. 'Your waiting days are over, your dreams a reality.'

Peace came in 1945.

Wealth and Power

The Liberal Party governed for the first eleven years of the new century. Votes among the working class, however, began to shift further to the left, towards socialism. A Socialist Party was formed in 1901. 'Land and all the instruments of production,' promised the party, 'shall be owned and managed by the people.' Socialists felt strong. Workers in many towns felt excited about their chances of challenging capitalism successfully.

Landowners, farmers and the conservative middle class gathered around another new party, the Reform Party. They won power in 1912, ending the long government of the Liberals.

A class war then followed between the government and the left of the working class.

New Zealand suffering from sadness, First World War. **Gordon Calman**, Roll of Honour.

state. The share of national income pocketed by the richest one per cent of people fell from fifty-one per cent to a mere ten per cent, and while the rich got less rich, the poor got a lot less poor. The share of all private wealth owned by the poorest half of society increased by about 400 per cent in only two generations.

New Zealand, even more than before, claimed to be the 'heaven' of the working class.

People

New Zealand during the early 20th century was still controlled by the children or grandchildren of settlers from Britain, Ireland, Germany and Scandinavia. Laws were still based on a belief in the country as a new and 'better' Britain. Chinese people kept coming, but in very small groups. India was the homeland of other small groups of new settlers. Indians worked for wages, or set up shops. Governments for twenty years after the turn of the century passed tighter laws to try to prevent settlement of the country by Chinese and Indians.

Ships brought 120,000 new settlers during the first fifteen years of the century. One in three came from Australia, where economic growth was slower than New Zealand. Almost all the others came from Britain. The Liberal government 'assisted' many, or in other words gave them free or cheap tickets to come from Britain. The policy was based, as before, on a belief that bringing in workers was a good way to invest the income of the state. New workers would provide labour for capitalists. They would help develop trade and industry.

The Reform Party continued the policy when it won control of the government. Socialists and many labour leaders were unhappy. The newspaper *Truth*, for example, said that the

ABOVE:
Christchurch. *New Zealand Railways Publicity Branch* (artist unknown).
ABOVE LEFT:
Summer holiday.
L C Mitchell, *Lake Waikaremoana*.

policy of 'the flooding of the labour market' meant that employers could not only 'resist the just demands of their employees' but also lower the wages.

The new people settled mostly in the North Island, for while the South Island was rich its economy and population grew less quickly. Auckland grew so fast it was now significantly larger than the largest southern city, Christchurch. Wellington grew quickly too, becoming larger than Dunedin.

The First World War ended the arrival of large numbers of settlers, although only temporarily. A big new wave came during the 1920s, almost all arriving straight from Britain. The dominion government once again spent money to bring them out. Socialists once again were unhappy. The policy of bringing in so many new people was careless and would cause social disaster, wrote one socialist newspaper.

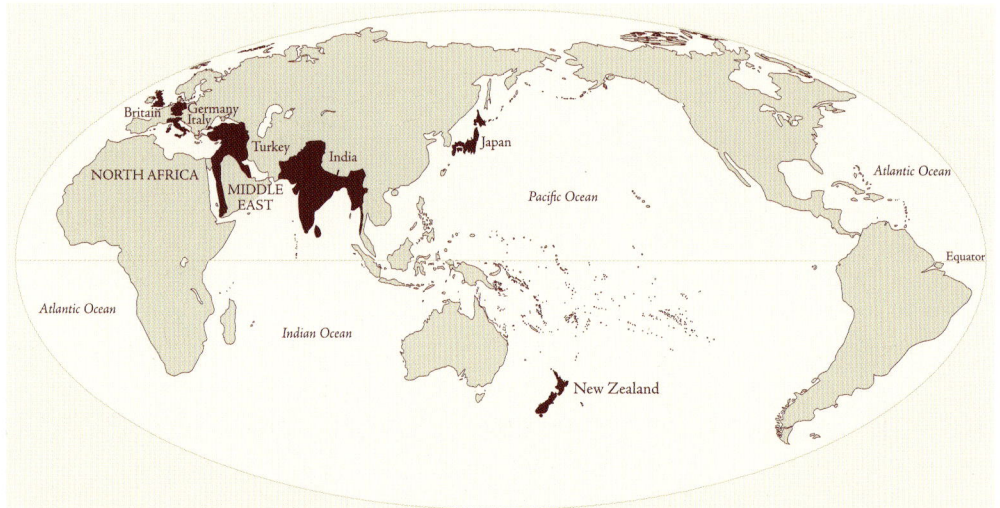

Auckland, the largest city in the dominion. *New Zealand Herald* (photographer unknown).

New Zealand in the World: immigrant homelands, enemies in war, 1900 to 1950

RIGHT:
A century after the Treaty of Waitangi.
FAR RIGHT:
New Zealand Shipping Company.

Fighting during the Second World War.
William Reed, *Jungle Patrol, Northern Solomons.*

Governments stopped helping new settlers only with the beginning of the Great Depression. People left the country in larger numbers than those arriving.

The beginning of the long boom from 1935 did not lead to a new wave of people coming to New Zealand. The Labour government, representing the working class, did not wish to help new settlers. They feared that such people would compete with workers for wages. The only exception was the welcoming of small groups of refugees. Germans were the biggest of these groups, more than a thousand coming to escape rule by the Nazi Party.

The Second World War, like the First World War, was a period when few people came into the country. The policy of a 'white New Zealand', however, began to end in a very quiet way. The tax on Chinese settlers imposed sixty years earlier was stopped. A few hundred Chinese people were invited to settle when the southern regions of their country were attacked by Japan.

After the Second World War the Labour and National governments provided tickets and other help for young workers to come to New Zealand. The two parties believed not only that more people were good for the economy but that the Pakeha population must increase to keep the country 'white'. The great majority of settlers were British. One new group of people came from the Netherlands; within twenty years more than 20,000 of them had settled in the country. They, like Germans and Scandinavians in the 19th century, lived in ways very similar to those of the British.

'I grew up understanding Dutch but speaking only English,' wrote Ragini Werner, who came from the Netherlands as a child. 'I soon turned into a proper little New Zealander.'

At the beach during the Second World War. **Evelyn Page**, *New Year Holiday (Corsair Bay)*.

Maori were still a small minority. Yet they had survived wars and the diseases brought by the new people. Maori numbers grew from the beginning of the 20th century. A belief widely held by Pakeha was that the two peoples enjoyed a good relationship. Maori art and songs were used as symbols of the country by governments, newspapers and advertising. Maori certainly had some power in the state. The Young Maori Party, a group of skilful politicians, was important in parliament. Apirana Ngata, for example, on several occasions acted as assistant prime minister at a time when it was impossible for a 'native' to hold such a powerful position in the governments of Australia, Canada or the United States.

The Young Maori Party was led by families holding high rank in traditional tribal society. The political opinions of such leaders were close, in many ways, to the opinions of the Pakeha leaders of the Reform Party. A democratic movement swept through Maori between the two world wars when a new religion was founded near Whanganui by a farm worker, Wiremu Ratana. The Ratana church was based on Christianity, led by ordinary men and women and spread quickly among many tribes. A political branch began to grow strong.

PEOPLE, PEOPLE, PEOPLE

City life, 1930s.
Russell Clark,
Saturday Night.

The Ratana movement within twelve years won all the Maori seats in parliament, linking itself with the Labour Party.

Almost all Maori were very poor. Eight out of ten Maori houses in one region were 'low-lying and damp', according to an official survey. Tribes lived in villages on their own small pieces of family land. On this land they grew grain and potatoes, and each household kept a few sheep, some pigs, perhaps a cow or two. Work was done in family groups. Young women and men went away from the villages every year to work for wages on Pakeha farms and estates, but then came home to the village to share the money.

'We had cows, we had pigs, we had everything — but no money!' said the daughter of one village family.

Maori and Pakeha often were happy to trade, talk, make friends, make love and marry one another, as always. The children in nearly every Maori village now were a mixture of Maori and Pakeha. Yet they still had a strong sense of being Maori. Maori were a culture, a way of life, a way of seeing the world.

Women and Men

The legal rights of women grew stronger thanks to several new laws in the first half of the century. Ordinary life, on the other hand, still was based on a belief that women and men should behave in certain ways.

Politicians, doctors, editors and advertisement writers nearly all were men who saw the best society as one where a woman devoted herself to working inside the house and bringing up children, while a man went out of the home to work for a wage or salary. The state spent money trying to encourage women to give birth to more babies in order to increase the number of workers, soldiers and mothers of tomorrow. The National Coalition in 1917 passed a law ordering all girls in state schools to be taught sewing and cooking. Labour in 1936 passed a law setting a minimum wage for men that would be enough to house, feed and care for three children and a wife. The concept of the 'family wage' had become central to state policy.

Yet behaviour still kept changing. Sex before marriage was widespread. One out of every three women was pregnant before her wedding day. Also, women were not willing to give in to the pressure of the state when deciding to have or not to have a baby. Women practised birth control effectively during the late 19th and early 20th century. The average birth rate fell in forty years from seven to only three children for every married woman. The concept of the 'family wage' did not stop more and more women from leaving the home to take paid work. Young women from the working class always had taken on tasks for wages. Young women of the middle class now got jobs. At the start of the century only two per cent of the growing number of women in paid work were employed as office staff; their strength had jumped to forty per cent by the middle of the century.

The state, while during years of peace trying to make women see themselves as wives and mothers, behaved the opposite way during years of war. War governments pushed women into wage or salary work, or volunteer work. Women of the middle class crowded the streets to raise money for soldiers during the First World War. Often they dressed in 'drag', men's clothing, wearing trousers for the first time in the history of New Zealand. Sir Joseph Ward, one of the leaders of the National Coalition, told parliament that the war had 'altered the whole aspect of what is due to the women of the world'. Women were rewarded with the right to sit in parliament. Women and men now stood almost at the same level under the law.

Women campaigned for election to parliament, although none won until 1933, when working-class citizens in one district voted for Elizabeth McCombs. A woman became a minister in government in 1947, when Mabel Howard became Minister of Social Welfare.

Women with babies. **Olivia Spencer Bower**, *Rawene Mothers*.

The Second World War led to even more of a revolution in the lives of women than the First World War. Young single women often were forced to work on farms or in city industry. One out of three wage and salary workers, by the end of the war, was a woman. Thousands of other women chose to go into the army, air force or navy.

Men who had sex with men, meanwhile, were still outside the law. Charles Mackay, gay mayor of Whanganui, was so afraid of people learning the truth about his secret sex life that he shot a fellow gay man, the poet D'Arcy Cresswell. Frank Sargeson, a leading short story writer of the mid 20th century, was tried in court for having sex with the artist Leonard Hollobon.

Women who had sex with women, while not seen as criminals, were not acceptable to most people. Frances Hodgkins, perhaps the most brilliant New Zealand painter of her generation, kept secret her sex life with other women, among them another painter, Dorothy Richmond. Katherine Mansfield, the famous writer, kept secret her sexual experiences with other women too. She left the country forever after her father read a story she wrote about lesbian love. Other secret lesbians were the poet Ursula Bethell and the first woman to climb Mount Cook, Freda Du Faur. Two young women were convicted in 1946 for marrying each other; one of them had hidden her true identity and pretended to be a man. Lesbians and gay men did not find life easy.

The Best Little Country in the World

The lives of most people quickly grew crowded with more and more goods after the Second World War. Cars, rubber, radio, film, plastics and electrical goods seemed to give everything a new speed, a new shine. Suburbs, street after street of new houses, spread for kilometres around every city. The ordinary wage worker now could buy a new house with big windows. Rows and rows of such houses were built along the streets of the new suburbs.

Writers and artists, as before, wondered about the meaning of this wealth, and what people chose to buy. The dream of New Zealanders, claimed novelist Bill Pearson, was a boring dream in which everyone wanted to be equal with everyone else and to live in a state of security.

'Everybody acts the same, receives the same amount of the world's goods, everyone moves in the same direction. Everyone has simple tastes.'

'The best little country in the world,' said others.

Welfare state. The Labour Party saw family life as the heart of the welfare state and society.
The National Party, as this political advertisement shows, also saw family life as the heart of society.

A Family Affair

NEW ZEALAND

SIX
Suburbs, 1950 to 2000

Peace

New Zealand during the last half of the 20th century enjoyed more peace than it had for many centuries of its history. The 17th and 18th centuries had been a time when blood flowed during tribal wars. The 19th century had been torn apart by the Musket Wars and the New Zealand Wars. The First World War and the Second World War had led to awful suffering during the first half of the 20th century.

Now, however, the country was remarkably peaceful.

A 'Cold War' was fought during the 1950s and 1960s between capitalist states and the socialist nations, mostly a war of words but sometimes real fighting. Two treaties were signed, by which New Zealand became an ally of the United States. New Zealand governments did not want to get involved too deeply in the conflicts of that time, however, and therefore took care to send only small military forces to wars in Malaysia, Korea and Vietnam. Citizens disagreed with one another during the late 1960s over whether or not to support the United States in the Vietnam War. A Labour government, elected in 1972, withdrew from that war. A later Labour government, elected in 1984, stopped being an ally of the United States. The army for the last quarter of the century was very small. Governments used it mostly in 'peace keeping' work for the United Nations.

Peace, however, did not always go with a feeling that the nation was happy.

The long boom continued for thirty years after the end of the Second World War. New Zealanders earned more and more money. The welfare state guaranteed that the money was shared quite fairly between all social groups. Yet the incomes of other western countries grew faster than New Zealand. The long boom came to an end everywhere in the western world in the middle of the 1970s and afterwards the economy went through a quarter of a century of ups and downs, rather like the ten years after the First World War. Wages for the average working man began to drop as soon as the boom stopped. Wages for the average working woman began to shrink during the 1980s, together with a further drop in wages for the average working man. Never in the history of the country had wages fallen so steadily for so long.

New Zealand in 1960. **Dennis Beytagh**.

Vietnam War. **Jeffrey Harris**, *My Lai*.

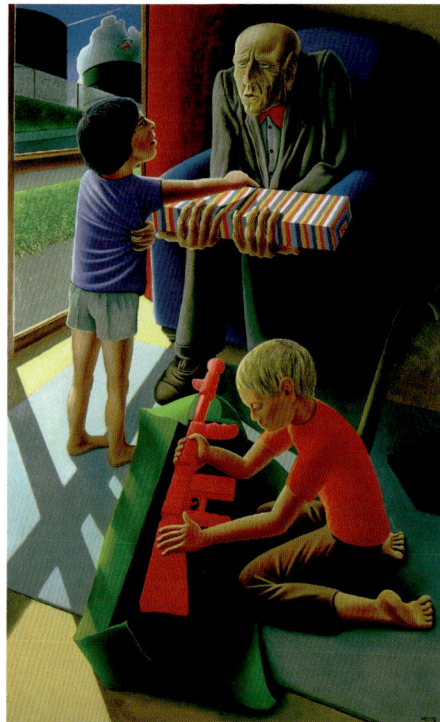

The incomes of most people rose in the middle of the 1990s, beginning another boom period of about fifteen years in which the average wage and salary grew steadily. Yet twenty or so other western nations now enjoyed higher average incomes than New Zealand.

New Zealand citizens, for the first time in their history as a state, knew that they were now not one of the richest peoples in the world.

Power

Falling behind in a race to be rich was not a bad thing. New Zealand still had plenty of money. The wealth of the nation was more than enough for everybody to enjoy good housing, good food, good health and a life not only good but happy and satisfying.

The last two decades of the century, however, saw national wealth shared less fairly.

Political power during most of the 1950s and 1960s was held by the National Party. National kept the welfare state. Wealth and income were shared out between the middle class and the working class more equally than in nearly any other country in the world. The willingness of the National Party to support the welfare state was surprising, in some ways. National often claimed to oppose state involvement in the economy and in society. The party certainly was supported by nearly the whole of the capitalist class; the working class voted for the Labour Party. The peak of the welfare state came during the late 1970s and early 1980s under a National government led by Robert Muldoon.

New Zealand seemed strongly committed to social democracy.

Yet the welfare state was attacked suddenly, in the middle of the 1980s, by a completely new policy begun under a government of the Labour Party. The economic policies were called

Working class man.
Garth Tapper,
Southdown Boy.

'Rogernomics', after Roger Douglas, Minister of Finance. They were the complete opposite of traditional policies of Labour. Citizens were amazed. The political right was happy. The political left was shocked.

'Rogernomics,' wrote one citizen, 'transformed New Zealand from a society into an economy'. The policy frightened many, above all the working class.

Labour lost power in 1990 but the new policy grew stronger under government by the National Party. Ruth Richardson, Minister of Finance, was the first woman in New Zealand history to hold such a senior rank in a government. National economic policy came to be known as 'Ruthanasia', playing on the word 'euthanasia', which means killing someone who has an incurable disease.

Ruthanasia and Rogernomics were based on a belief that the state should not be involved in the economy. A welfare state was said to make a weak economy. The economy should be left to the 'free market'. Otherwise the economy would become less and less efficient, and citizens as a whole would have less and less wealth.

State support for farmers and factory owners was taken away. The state sold much of its own property: railways, airlines, the postal system, electricity, telecommunications, insurance and banking. New Zealand became one of the least protected economies in the capitalist world. Welfare benefits were made smaller, even though more people needed such benefits. The working conditions of those earning a wage or salary were opened to

Young woman dreaming. **Ian Scott**, *Leapaway Girl*.

'the market'. Capitalists were given greater freedom to force employees to work long hours, with worse conditions, than under the welfare state.

Tax law changed dramatically. The rate of tax paid by those earning the highest incomes quickly became lower than in almost any other capitalist country. The poor, on the other hand, were taxed. Tax on citizens who earned the lowest incomes had begun for the first time in history under the National government of the 1970s. The Labour government of the 1980s established a new system of indirect tax on goods and services. Tax was now being used as a way to take money from the poor in order to take less from the rich.

Rogernomics and Ruthanasia were meant to cause economic growth. Yet growth was not very striking. A large number of people now had no jobs.

'Curtains were drawn in houses as people felt the shame,' said one of them, Ngahiwi Tomoana.

The end of the strong welfare state meant that a wide gap quickly opened between rich and poor. The gap opened everywhere in the western world during the last twenty years of the 20th century. Yet the western nation in which the difference between the incomes of people at the top and at the bottom of society grew most quickly was New Zealand. The wealth gap by the end of the century was worse than in the European Union, Australia and Canada.

A wide gap in wealth led to a wide gap in health. The people of rich suburbs by the end of the century lived to an average age of about 90 years, while the people of the poorest suburbs died on average before the age of 65 years, according to the state health ministry.

So the end of the welfare state not only made the rich richer, but it began killing the poor.

People

New Zealand doubled its population to about four million people during the second half of the century. Population growth was much the same as during the previous half century. Women were even less willing than before to have many babies, however, controlling their family size more and more firmly. People came from elsewhere in the world to make up for the lack of births. The biggest wave came during the thirty years of economic boom after the Second World War. A majority of those people were from Britain, but a striking new step was taken as more and more workers were needed than could be found among the people of Europe. The National government decided to welcome 'brown' workers from the neighbouring islands of Polynesia.

The Second Polynesian Settlement began, about seven hundred years after the First Polynesian Settlement. The people of Samoa, Niue and the Cook Islands lived in colonies of New Zealand. They arrived in the tens of thousands, looking for high wages. They found work mostly in industry. Albert Wendt, one of the leading writers to grow up in the new world of Polynesian New Zealand, wrote about a settler from Samoa.

During the man's first four weeks in the factory he worked at odd jobs. ... He was afraid in the factory. Caught up in the noise and the overwhelming size of the building, the intricate system of machines ... the large number of workers whose language he didn't understand, he felt small and lost.

Polynesian communities grew in the suburbs of some cities, especially in Auckland.

A new Labour government after 1972 made another major change in policy. The citizens of any country in the world now were invited to come to New Zealand. New people were allowed entry on the basis not of their race or culture but their schooling, their savings and their skills.

Pakeha worried by the end of the long boom began leaving New Zealand. Polynesians kept coming into New Zealand. Vietnamese settlers were welcomed, too, together with smaller groups from Cambodia and Laos. Other groups of people came during the late 1980s and all the 1990s, mostly from China, Taiwan, Korea and Japan. South Asians from India and Sri Lanka then arrived in numbers equal to the East Asians. Settlers came from

Polynesians in the suburbs.
Mark Adams,
Mrs Suluape at Paul Suluape's Sister Kalala's Place, Mangere, South Auckland, 24.3.1985.

New Zealand in the
World: immigrant
homelands, 1950 to
2000

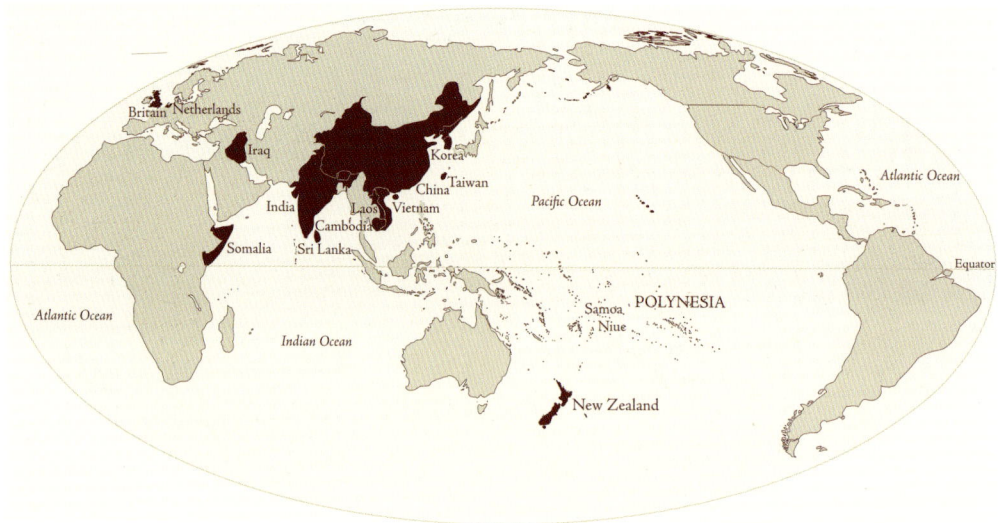

Somalia and Iraq. By the end of the century nearly 700,000 people living in New Zealand
had been born outside the country. They and their children had varying experiences of life
in the new land.

'I enjoy being Chinese,' wrote Chun Wei-sing. 'On the negative side, I do still have to
deal with those who consider Chinese and other Asians to be inferior.' 'The local people are
very friendly,' wrote Jinli, who came from Beijing to live in Christchurch.

A 'white' land had become a 'multicultural' land, a land whose people belonged to many
races and cultures. One in fifteen people by the end of the century was Asian. One in fifteen
people was Polynesian. Artists, musicians, writers and everybody else among the new
groups had new thoughts and new feelings about what it was to be a New Zealander.

Maori also developed a wide range of new thoughts and feelings about what it was to be
a New Zealander.

Maori history up to the middle of the 20th century was a history of people who nearly
always lived in country villages. Almost all were farmers, or farm workers, and were poor.
Maori after the Second World War moved to city suburbs. Almost all now worked for a
wage. New generations of children, growing up in the suburbs, worked in industry and in
growing numbers began to get jobs as clerks or in professions, earning a salary.

Maori population grew quickly. At the end of the Second World War about 100,000
people were Maori. At the end of the century the total was about 600,000, of whom one
in six lived in Australia. The exact numbers are not known, because sexual relationships
between races had become so common that nobody now was entirely Maori.

The move to the cities and the growth in numbers led to a sense of strength and a new

Land, sky and history. **Brent Wong**, *untitled*.

energy. Maori began to claim a bigger share of power and wealth. They demanded, too, that the state obey the Treaty of Waitangi. Maori protest was so successful that the treaty began to be applied to the laws. A key step came with the Waitangi Tribunal, established in 1975 and after ten years given strong powers. Land, forests and money began to be handed over by the state. The two tribes of Tainui and Ngai Tahu, for example, were each given $170 million to make good the land stolen from them in the past by the government of New Zealand.

Maori gained in many other ways. A growing political strength was shown in elections to parliament. Maori were elected to fifteen seats in parliament in 1996, the majority being chosen by citizens who mostly were not Maori. Pakeha, Asians and Polynesians, in other words, were willing to choose Maori to represent them in the national capital.

Women and Men

Women also claimed a much greater role in the economy and society. The late years of the 19th century had made women and men almost equal under law. Laws kept changing, slowly, during the early 20th century. Change became very striking in the second half of the century.

A 'sexual revolution' swept through the western world, based on a belief that women and men should enjoy wide freedom in their love lives. The last years of the long boom swept away nearly all other points of view. 'Make love, not war,' said many young people. Women as never before freely entered and left marriage and sexual relationships. They had fewer and fewer babies. Women walked more confidently through the streets, challenged men more openly, and spoke out.

Protest and other movements founded by women from the late 1960s led to wide changes. Women won equal pay with men when working for a wage or salary. New laws improved their protection from violent lovers and husbands. Women rose to the very top of power. Five of the six highest positions in the state were in the hands of women by the end of the century. The prime minister was Helen Clark. She had replaced another woman prime minister, Jennifer Shipley. New Zealand was the first country in the world where women followed each other as prime ministers.

Not only women but other groups of people won new rights. Men who wanted men as their sexual partners fought for freedom under law. A Gay Liberation Front was formed in 1971 and within three years parliament began discussing giving men the right to have sexual relationships with one another. Robin Duff, openly gay, stood for election to parliament the following year. *Squeeze*, the first gay film ever made in the country, screened four years later, and in 1986 parliament passed a Homosexual Law Reform Act. The new law gave men freedom to have sex with other men. A law in 1993 made the reform stronger by giving further protection to the rights of gays.

Open and relaxed laws had been agreed upon by most people in the country as the best basis for society.

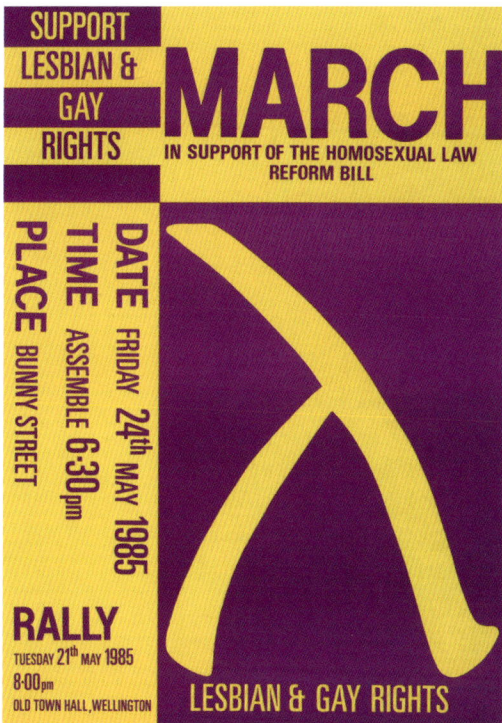

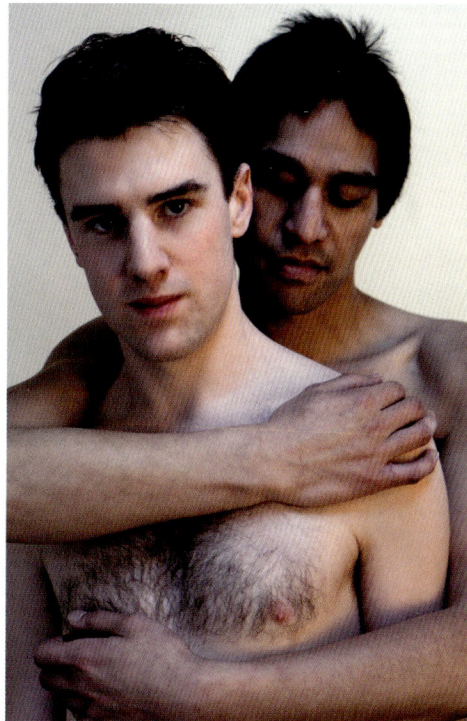

LEFT and FAR LEFT: Gay history. A poster advising of a rally in support of the Homosexual Law Reform Bill and a promotional photograph for *Mates and Lovers*, a theatre work by **Ronald Trifero Nelson** exploring the history of gay New Zealand. The actors shown here are Simon K Leary and Paora Taurima.

Yet the lives of homosexual men were still hard, in some ways. A study of young people at the end of the century found that gay boys were far more likely than other boys to be treated badly, and to kill themselves. Women, too, had won legal but not truly equal status. Gains were very strong in politics, education and the professions; they were weak in business and industry. Only seven per cent of directors in the hundred biggest companies in the country were women, and only one in five editors of major newspapers.

A New Century

New Zealand kept certain basic values throughout the late 20th century and now keeps those values early in the 21st century. The way of life is less formal than in nearly any other western country. A belief in 'easy going' behaviour means that most people treat each other as fellow citizens rather than as people of high or low status. New Zealand is one of the most honest and least corrupt lands in the world. The nation is also, according to various surveys, among the two or three places where people enjoy the most freedom in the world.

What does the 21st century hold in store for New Zealand?

Peace, almost certainly. The experience of two world wars early last century gave rise to a

Indian New Zealand. *Krishnan's Dairy* first appeared on stage in 1997 and was written by **Jacob Rajan** and **Justin Lewis**. The play explores the lives of Indian New Zealanders. The actor shown here is Jacob Rajan.

Chinese New Zealand. *My Wedding and Other Secrets*, a film written and directed by **Roseanne Liang**, tells the story of the relationship between two young New Zealanders, one white and one Chinese. The actors shown here are Michelle Ang and Matt Whelan.

strong belief in peace among most people in the country. New Zealand has no enemy. New Zealand for many years will probably not seek any military ally. Voters will probably remain willing to support only a very small army and a tiny air force and navy.

Wealth, almost certainly. A moderate wealth, in which not only the middle class but the working class of the country continue to enjoy incomes more than enough to afford comfort for nearly everybody. Average wages are not very good any more, by the standards of the western world. Yet many people in the country believe that there are more important things than money.

'I do not measure my life in terms of the things I own,' wrote a citizen early in the new century. 'New Zealanders are smarter than that. Enjoy life. Ride your bike. Read a book.'

The typical citizen reads more books than the people of nearly any other country.

A multicultural society, definitely. The nation is no longer 'white New Zealand'. Pakeha, Polynesians, Asians and Africans share the country. Asians within another twenty years will outnumber Maori. They may well, by the end of the century, outnumber everybody. The various groups are marrying one another, too. Marriage has always been common between Pakeha, Maori and Polynesian. Marriage now is becoming common between Pakeha and Asians. The children of the future will often be of mixed race and mixed culture.

A society based on equal opportunity for everybody?

New Zealanders nearly all believed, from the late 1880s to the early 1980s, that a good goal for the country was equal opportunity. The belief grew weaker during the last twenty years of the 20th century. A wide gap now divides rich and poor. The gap, as yet, is not as wide as during the 19th century. Will citizens come to a new agreement that society should be based permanently on such a wide gap? Or will there be another change in mood, and a new movement towards equal opportunity?

Glossary

Aotearoa	the North Island of New Zealand; often used now to mean the whole of New Zealand
hapu	group of several families
iwi	tribe; group of hapu
kiore	type of rat
kumara	sweet potato
kuri	dog
mana	authority and status
mere	type of weapon
pa	village protected with wooden walls
Pakeha	Europeans; white people; people who are not Maori
patu	type of weapon
pipi	type of shellfish
Polynesia	the islands of the eastern and southern Pacific
Polynesians	the people of Polynesia
taiaha	type of spear
Te Ika-a-Maui	the North Island of New Zealand
Te Waipounamu	the South Island of New Zealand
ti	type of tree
utu	revenge; balance
waka	type of boat

Picture Credits

p. 27 L C Mitchell, *A Reconstruction of the Signing of the Treaty of Waitangi*. A-242-002.

pp. 28–29 John Wallace, *View of Wellington Harbour from Thorndon Beach*. B-079-007.

p. 32 Edward Ashworth, *Scene Near the Barracks*. E-042-006.

p. 33 W H Speer, *New Zealand Digger*. E-395-033.

p. 35 Cyprian Bridge, *Sketch of the Action at Mawe, New Zealand, on the 8th May, 1845*. A-079-008.

p. 38 C D Barraud, *Cheviot Hills Homestead*. NON-ATL-P-0083.

p. 42 *New Zealand Graphic and Ladies Journal*, The Benching Room of Sargood Son and Ewen's Factory, 1892. PUBL-0163-1892-003.

p. 43 *New Zealand Graphic and Ladies Journal*, The Machinery Room of Sargood Son and Ewen's Factory, 1892. PUBL-0163-1892-002.

p. 45 Philip Presants, *Young New Zealand at Play; Cricket in a Mining Town*. C-079-054.

p. 50 Gordon Calman, *Roll of Honour*. A-224-039.

p. 52 H M Moore-Jones, *To the memory of our hero comrade 'Murphy' (Simpson) killed May 1915*. C-057-002.

p. 55 *New Zealand Railways Publicity Branch, Christchurch, New Zealand South Island*. Eph-E-TOURISM-Christchurch-1935-01.

p. 55 L C Mitchell, *Lake Waikaremoana*. Eph-A-TOURISM-Waikaremoana-ca1930-02.

p. 56 *New Zealand Herald*, Queen Street, Auckland, 1929 (photographer unknown). PAColl-0267-03.

p. 56 A century after the Treaty of Waitangi. Eph-E-TOURISM-1940-01.

p. 56 New Zealand Shipping Company. Eph-H-SHIP-1930s-01.

p. 63 New Zealand National Party, *A Family Affair*. Eph-A-NZ-NATIONAL-1949-01-cover.

p. 75 Homosexual law reform. Eph-C-GAY-1985-03.

Auckland War Memorial Museum

p. 36 Gustavus von Tempsky, *British Camp Surprised by Maoris who were Driven off with Heavy Losses*. PD29(1-8).

Gareth Watkins, photographer

p. 75 Photograph from the play *Mates and Lovers*, based on the book *Mates and Lovers: A History of Gay New Zealand* by Chris Brickell.

Hocken Collections, Uare Taoka o Hakena, University of Otago

pp. 1, 40–41 James Smetham, *The New Zealand Chiefs in Wesley's House*. 13,395.

p. 2, 30 William Fox, *St George's Bay, Auckland. Mr Blackett's House*. 82/63.

p. 3, 58 Evelyn Page, *New Year Holiday (Corsair Bay)*. 73200.

p. 31 J T Thomson, *Tuapeka Gold Rush, Otago 1861*. 92/1290.

p. 35 John Williams, *Ruapekapeka, N.Z. January 1846*. 12,544.

p. 39 A C Cooke, *Dunedin*. 22,616.

p. 47 G P Nerli, *Arthur Hadfield Fisher*. 24,060.0.

© Indian Ink Theatre Company

p. 76 *Krishnan's Dairy*.

Jae Frew, photographer. My Wedding and Other Secrets © 2010 South Pacific Pictures Ltd.

p. 77 *My Wedding and Other Secrets*.

Museum of New Zealand Te Papa Tongarewa

p. 3, 60 Olivia Spencer Bower, *Rawene Mothers*. 1993-0021-1.

p. 9 Alex Kennedy, *Model Tipaerua*. FE011788.

p. 19 T J Grant, *War Dance*. 1991-0003-16.

p. 39 Charles Blomfield, *Orakei Korako on the Waikato*. 1994-0012-1.

p. 39 James Nairn, *Tess*. 1939-0001-1.

p. 48 H Linley Richardson, *In Fancy Dress*. 1948-0005-3.

p. 57 William Reed, *Jungle Patrol, Northern Solomons*. 1992-0013-1.

p. 59 Russell Clark, *Saturday Night*. 1991-0024-1.

p. 66 Jeffrey Harris, *My Lai*. 1981-0021-1.

p. 67 Michael Smither, *Gifts*. 1980-0043-3.

p. 68 Garth Tapper, *Southdown Boy*. Reg no.?

p. 69 Ian Scott, *Leapaway Girl*. 1971-0023-1.

p. 71 Mark Adams, *Mrs Suluape at Paul Suluape's Sister Kalala's Place, Mangere, South Auckland, 24.3.1985*. O.004025.

p. 73 Brent Wong, *untitled*. 2001-0030-1. Reproduced courtesy of the artist, www.brentwong-painter.com.

Tourism New Zealand/Alexander Turnbull Library, Wellington, New Zealand

p. 64 Dennis Beytagh, *New Zealand*. Eph-E-TOURISM-1960-01.

Index